COOKIE CLASSICS
MADE EASY

One-Bowl Recipes

————— ✲✲ —————

Perfect Results

BRANDI SCALISE

PHOTOGRAPHY BY KATIE CRAIG

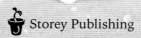

Storey Publishing

The mission of Storey Publishing is to serve our customers by publishing practical information that encourages personal independence in harmony with the environment.

Edited by Margaret Sutherland and Sarah Guare
Art direction and book design by Alethea Morrison
Indexed by Christine R. Lindemer, Boston Road Communications

Cover and interior photography by Katie Craig

Storey books are available for special premium and promotional uses and for customized editions. For further information, please call 1-800-793-9396.

Storey Publishing, 210 MASS MoCA Way, North Adams, MA 01247, www.storey.com

Printed in China by Toppan Leefung Printing Ltd.
10 9 8 7 6 5 4 3 2 1

Library of Congress Cataloging-in-Publication Data on file

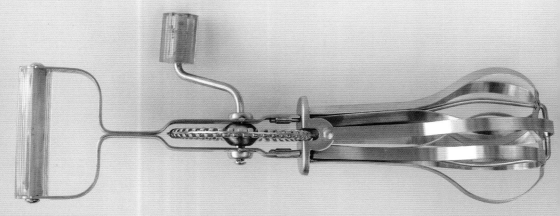

CONTENTS

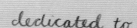

dedicated to

MY MOM: an amazing cook and baker. This woman makes an Italian red sauce that will always keep you coming back for more. As for her baking, at Christmas she fills the kitchen table so full of cookies that there's no room for anyone to sit. She then arranges them on cookie platters for all her friends and family.

MY DAD: who I can honestly say is the most amazing man I know. He has kept me in line all these years, and that hasn't been an easy task. I can be a little stubborn, have tunnel vision, and scare the socks off the man. He has always turned the tables and seen things from many perspectives. He's solid, stands by his word, and is someone you can rely on and trust. My dad has shown me how to be driven and have integrity. I love both my mom and dad so much.

MY BROTHERS: both of whom I have learned much from. Both are very creative and smart, and (I promised I would mention) how very handsome they are.

EVERYONE WHO HAS TOUCHED MY HEART and taught me in so many different ways: It may be something as small as someone saying to me, "When you walk by a person, look them in the eye and say hello." Or "They can't say yes if you don't ask." Big or small, no matter what, I love you all. My life wouldn't be the same without you.

AND MY BABY GIRL: my first taste tester. She has challenged my life in so many wonderful ways. I hope I can be someone for her to look up to. I love her more than anything.

INTRODUCTION

As the saying goes, "Life is what happens when you're busy making plans." Let's just say I'm a planner. I had thought that by the age of 25 I would be married with two children and have a Colonial-style house, a white picket fence, and a Volvo wagon. As life would have it, as I sit here writing this at the age of 40, I have never been married, and at the age of 35 I became a single mother to the most amazing little girl. I work full-time as a stylist and manager of my best friend's spa, I'm a landlord, and I have a small photography business. I also have an amazing support group consisting of family, friends, coworkers, guests of the spa who have become family over the years, and a wonderful boyfriend. My life is not as I had "planned" it (and come to find out, I don't even like Colonial-style houses!); regardless, I wouldn't change a thing.

When I was 29, I bought my first home. It was a two-family home; I had the upstairs and my tenants had the downstairs. For the very first time I had a full kitchen — my very own kitchen! I also had people to cook and bake for, which I was very excited about. I had a few cookbooks, but it made me crazy to see the recipes; in my eyes they were far too complicated. I wanted a straightforward cookbook that used as few utensils and dishes as possible. So, I decided to write a cookbook that would meet my own standards and make baking easier.

MY SIMPLE APPROACH

Over the years I have listened to people tell me how complicated and time-consuming it is to bake. When I explain to them what I do with my cookies, mixing everything in one bowl, they get excited. Most cookie recipes call for mixing the dry and wet ingredients separately, but I've found this isn't necessary. By adding the ingredients to the bowl in the order I've listed them, your dough will come together perfectly. It's easier and simpler, and you will have one less dish to clean!

You will fall in love all over again with baking, thanks to the simplicity of these recipes. Even if you have the busiest of schedules, you have time to whip up a batch of delicious cookies. In as little as 30 minutes, you can combine all your ingredients into one bowl, mix, bake, and come out looking like a gourmet baker. No time to bake? No problem. In about 10 minutes, you can make the dough (in the morning, at night, or whenever works for you) and pop it in the fridge; bake it within 24 hours.

I hope this book will make your life a little easier and a little sweeter.

INGREDIENTS AND TOOLS

This is where I make your life even simpler and tell you everything I used and where I found it.

MIXER: I use a KitchenAid electric stand mixer to put together my dough, and I highly recommend it. You could also use an electric hand mixer or just mix the dough by hand (if you have big muscles!).

OVEN: You can use any oven to bake these cookies. I have used three ovens (two regular electric ovens and one convection oven) to test these recipes, so the timing should be pretty accurate.

BUTTER: I have used both salted and unsalted butter in my cookies, and honestly, it doesn't make that much of a difference. If you like your food a little on the salty side, use salted butter; if not, use unsalted butter. Use what tastes good to you, and enjoy!

As for the temperature of the butter, if you have an electric mixer, like I do, you can use cold butter right from the fridge. If you're mixing by hand, it's best if the butter is at room temperature (it usually takes 30 minutes to 1 hour to soften when pulled from the fridge) or softened in the microwave. I never use melted butter; it makes flat cookies.

EXTRACTS: I use a lot of different extracts. You can buy some extracts at the grocery store, or shop online (I buy most of mine at www.beanilla.com).

NUTS, DRIED FRUIT, CARAMEL BITS, AND MARSHMALLOWS: If I can't find one of these products locally, I buy it online (I like www.nuts.com, www.nutsinbulk .com, and www.superiornut.com). Caramel bits have been a challenge for me to find. Nestlé has them, and I have bought them at www.nuts.com. As far as marshmallows, I use Kraft Jet-Puffed Mallow Bits. They come in a container like the kind that holds grated Parmesan cheese. The marshmallows look just like those you would find in a packet of hot chocolate. Or you can use regular old mini marshmallows. Just remember to use parchment paper when baking with them.

COOKIE SHEETS: I love my cookie sheets; they're nothing fancy. I use two Calphalon 12- by 17-inch cookie sheets that have a nonstick coating, making them a dream to bake cookies on. You could also use regular (*not* nonstick) cookie sheets and line them with parchment paper.

SCOOP AND SPATULA: I use a metal cookie scoop; it looks like a mini old-fashioned ice cream scooper. You can buy one just about anywhere. All of these recipes call for either a 1-inch or a $1\frac{1}{2}$-inch scoop. Metal is best, as the dough seems to stick to the plastic ones. If you don't have a cookie scoop, use a regular spoon to measure out heaping spoonfuls. I use a silicone spatula made by Prepology when I need to scrape the sides of the bowl. It is heat-resistant, so I can also use it for melting chocolate. I use a plastic spatula on my nonstick cookie sheets because metal would scratch them.

ALL-NIGHTER

Don't eat this cookie at night or you will have trouble falling asleep. This rich dark chocolate cookie with sweet-tart cranberries, crunchy macadamia nuts, and coffee has a ton of different flavors; it's like the Fourth of July in your mouth.

★ ★

1 cup (2 sticks) butter, room temperature

1 cup granulated sugar

1/2 cup firmly packed dark brown sugar

2 eggs

2 teaspoons vanilla extract

2 tablespoons instant coffee (I use Folgers)

1/4 teaspoon salt

3/4 teaspoon baking soda

2/3 cup unsweetened dark cocoa powder (I use Hershey's Special Dark)

2 cups all-purpose flour

2 cups semisweet chocolate chips

1/2 cup macadamia nuts

1/2 cup dried cranberries

1. Preheat the oven to 350°F/175°C. If you're not using nonstick cookie sheets, line them with parchment paper.

2. Combine the butter, granulated sugar, brown sugar, eggs, vanilla, instant coffee, salt, and baking soda in one large mixing bowl. Mix well, preferably with an electric mixer, occasionally scraping the sides of the bowl. Add the cocoa powder and mix, then add the flour and mix again. Add the chocolate chips, macadamia nuts, and cranberries, and mix well.

3. Using a 1½-inch cookie scoop or a large rounded teaspoon, scoop out the dough and drop about 1½ inches apart on the cookie sheets.

4. Bake for 13 to 15 minutes, until you can smell a wonderful chocolate aroma filling the air. Transfer to a wire rack and let cool.

Makes about 3 dozen cookies

BERKSHIRE ROAD

Just like rocky road ice cream, this cookie has a rich chocolate
flavor with almonds, chocolate chips, and marshmallows.

* *

1 cup (2 sticks) butter, room
    temperature

1 cup granulated sugar

1/2 cup firmly packed dark brown
    sugar

2 eggs

1/4 teaspoon salt

3/4 teaspoon baking soda

1/4 cup milk

2 teaspoons vanilla extract

2 1/2 cups all-purpose flour

2/3 cup unsweetened cocoa powder

2 cups semisweet chocolate chips

1 cup chopped almonds

1 cup mini marshmallows

1 cup white chocolate chips

1. Preheat the oven to 375°F/190°C. Line two
   cookie sheets with parchment paper.

2. Combine the butter, granulated sugar, brown
   sugar, eggs, salt, baking soda, milk, and vanilla
   in a large mixing bowl. Mix well, preferably
   with an electric mixer. Add the flour and cocoa
   powder and mix until well combined, occasionally scraping the sides of the bowl. Add the
   semisweet chocolate chips, almonds, marshmallows, and white chocolate chips, and mix
   once more until combined.

3. Using a 1½-inch cookie scoop or a large
   rounded tablespoon, scoop out the dough and
   place about 1 inch apart on the parchment-lined
   cookie sheets.

4. Bake for 12 to 15 minutes, until you can smell
   a wonderful chocolate aroma filling the air.
   Transfer to a wire rack and let cool.

Makes about 3 dozen cookies

BRITTANY'S S'MORES

These cookies are a lot less messy than your traditional s'mores yet are still packed with all the flavor!

— ★ ★ —

½ cup (1 stick) butter, room temperature

1 cup creamy Biscoff spread

3 eggs

1 cup firmly packed light brown sugar

1 cup granulated sugar

1 cup broken graham crackers

1 teaspoon vanilla extract

1 teaspoon baking soda

1 teaspoon baking powder

2½ cups all-purpose flour

1 cup semisweet chocolate chips

1 cup mini marshmallows

½ cup white chocolate chips

1. Preheat the oven to 355°F/180°C. Line two cookie sheets with parchment paper.

2. Combine the butter, Biscoff spread, eggs, brown sugar, granulated sugar, graham crackers, vanilla, baking soda, and baking powder in a large mixing bowl. Mix well, preferably with an electric mixer. Add the flour and mix well, scraping the sides of the bowl if needed. Add the semisweet chocolate chips, marshmallows, and white chocolate chips, and mix once more until everything is combined.

3. Using a 1½-inch cookie scoop or a large rounded tablespoon, measure out your dough, then squeeze each scoop into a ball. Place the balls of dough about 1 inch apart on the parchment-lined cookie sheets.

4. Bake for 12 to 15 minutes, until the edges are golden brown. Let cool for a bit on the cookie sheets, then transfer to a wire rack and let cool fully.

Makes about 4 dozen cookies

BY THE CAMPFIRE

These decadent little no-bake bundles of flavor will not last long.
They have a tendency to disappear into the darkness.

— ★ ★ —

- 1/2 cup (1 stick) butter, room temperature
- 1 1/2 cups creamy Biscoff spread
- 2 cups confectioners' sugar
- 1 1/2 cups mini marshmallows
- 4 large Hershey's bars, broken into pieces, or 16 ounces of your favorite melting chocolate

1. Line a large lidded container with parchment paper. The container should be large enough to hold all of the balls in a single layer.

2. Combine the butter, Biscoff spread, confectioners' sugar, and marshmallows in a large mixing bowl. Mix well, occasionally scraping the sides of the bowl.

3. Using a 1-inch cookie scoop or a rounded teaspoon, measure out the s'mores mixture. Roll the mixture into balls using the palms of your hands. Place the balls in the prepared container and chill overnight.

4. Place the Hershey's bar pieces in the top of a double boiler and melt over medium heat. Make sure you remove the chocolate from the heat as soon as it is fully melted. Or place the chocolate pieces in a microwave-safe bowl and heat in the microwave for 30-second intervals, stirring the chocolate after each interval, until all of the chocolate is melted.

5. Insert a wooden skewer into one chilled s'mores ball. Dip the ball into the melted chocolate, place back in the parchment-lined container, then remove the skewer. Leave the cookie with the hole from the skewer visible or, using a small spoon or the skewer itself, drizzle the melted chocolate onto the exposed surface to cover the hole. Repeat for the remaining s'mores balls.

6. Place the chocolate-covered balls in the refrigerator until the chocolate is set, 2 to 4 hours. Serve chilled.

Makes about 3½ dozen cookies

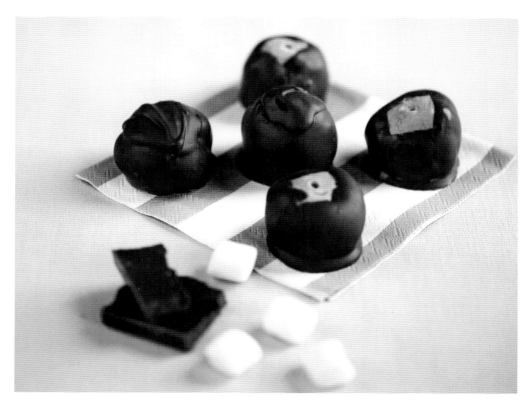

CARAMEL BY THE SEA

This cookie draws you in with its rich chocolate and sweet caramel,
then packs a punch with its bold sea salt.

* *

1 cup (2 sticks) butter, room
   temperature

1 cup plus 2 teaspoons granulated
   sugar

1/2 cup firmly packed dark brown
   sugar

2 eggs

1/2 teaspoon baking soda

1/2 teaspoon baking powder

1 teaspoon coarse sea salt

1 teaspoon vanilla extract

1/2 cup unsweetened cocoa powder

2 cups all-purpose flour

1 cup coarsely chopped pecans

1 cup caramel bits

1 cup semisweet chocolate chips

1 teaspoon finely ground sea salt

1. Preheat the oven to 350°F/175°C. Line two
   cookie sheets with parchment paper.

2. Combine the butter, 1 cup of the granulated
   sugar, brown sugar, eggs, baking soda, baking
   powder, coarse sea salt, and vanilla in a large
   mixing bowl. Mix well, preferably with an
   electric mixer, scraping the sides of the bowl if
   needed. Add the cocoa powder and flour, and
   mix again. Add the pecans, caramel bits, and
   chocolate chips, and mix one more time until
   all the ingredients are well combined.

3. Combine the finely ground sea salt and remaining 2 teaspoons granulated sugar in a small bowl.

4. Using a 1½-inch cookie scoop or a large rounded
   tablespoon, scoop out the dough and place about
   1 inch apart on the cookie sheets. Sprinkle the
   dough with the salt and sugar combination.

5. Bake for 15 to 18 minutes, until you can smell
   a wonderful chocolate aroma filling the air.
   Transfer to a wire rack and let cool.

Makes about 3½ dozen cookies

CHOCOLATE ALMOND COCONUT

In the mood for an Almond Joy candy bar? This is your cookie!

★ ★

1/2 cup (1 stick) butter, room temperature

1/2 cup vegetable oil

1/2 cup light corn syrup

1/2 cup firmly packed dark brown sugar

1 cup granulated sugar

2 eggs

1/2 teaspoon salt

2 teaspoons baking powder

1 teaspoon baking soda

1 tablespoon vanilla extract

1/4 cup milk or cream

1 tablespoon coconut extract

2/3 cup unsweetened cocoa powder

1 cup packed coconut flakes

3 1/2 cups all-purpose flour

1 cup coarsely chopped almonds

1. Preheat the oven to 350°F/175°C. If you're not using nonstick cookie sheets, line them with parchment paper.

2. Combine the butter, vegetable oil, corn syrup, brown sugar, granulated sugar, eggs, salt, baking powder, baking soda, vanilla, milk, and coconut extract in a large mixing bowl. Mix well, preferably with an electric mixer, occasionally scraping the sides of the bowl. Add the cocoa powder, coconut flakes, flour, and almonds, and mix until well combined.

3. Using a 1½-inch cookie scoop or a large rounded teaspoon, scoop out the dough and place about 1 inch apart on the cookie sheets.

4. Bake for 13 to 15 minutes, until you can smell a wonderful chocolate aroma filling the air. Transfer to a wire rack and let cool.

Makes about 4½ dozen cookies

CHOCOLATE RASPBERRY

This elegant chocolate-raspberry cookie has two incredible flavors that are bold yet complementary. It simply melts in your mouth.

— ＊ ＊ —

1 cup (2 sticks) butter, room temperature

1 cup firmly packed light brown sugar

2 eggs

1 teaspoon baking powder

1/2 teaspoon salt

1 tablespoon honey

1 generous tablespoon raspberry extract

2/3 cup Hershey's Special Dark unsweetened cocoa powder

2 cups all-purpose flour

2 cups semisweet chocolate chips

1. Preheat the oven to 365°F/185°C. If you're not using nonstick cookie sheets, line them with parchment paper.

2. Combine the butter, brown sugar, eggs, baking powder, salt, honey, and raspberry extract in a large mixing bowl. Mix well, preferably with an electric mixer, occasionally scraping the sides of the bowl. Add the cocoa powder and flour, and mix until everything is combined. Add the chocolate chips and mix again.

3. Using a 1-inch cookie scoop or a rounded teaspoon, scoop out the dough and drop 1 inch apart onto the cookie sheets.

4. Bake for 16 to 18 minutes, until you can smell a wonderful chocolate aroma filling the air. Transfer to a wire rack and let cool.

Makes about 4½ dozen cookies

CHOCOLATE REESE'S PEANUT BUTTER

This cookie reminds me of a Friendly's Reese's Pieces sundae. Add some vanilla ice cream and you just might have something.

— * * —

½ cup (1 stick) butter, room temperature

½ cup vegetable oil

1 cup crunchy peanut butter

3 eggs

1 cup firmly packed light brown sugar

1 cup granulated sugar

1 teaspoon vanilla extract

1 teaspoon baking soda

1 teaspoon baking powder

⅔ cup unsweetened cocoa powder

3 cups all-purpose flour

½ cup half-and-half

1½ cups Reese's Pieces

¾ cup semisweet chocolate chips

1. Preheat the oven to 355°F/180°C. If you're not using nonstick cookie sheets, line them with parchment paper.

2. Combine the butter, vegetable oil, peanut butter, eggs, brown sugar, granulated sugar, vanilla, baking soda, and baking powder in a large mixing bowl. Mix well, preferably with an electric mixer, occasionally scraping the sides of the bowl. Add the cocoa powder, flour, and half-and-half. Mix well, then add the Reese's Pieces and chocolate chips, and mix until well blended.

3. Using a 1½-inch cookie scoop or a large rounded teaspoon, scoop out the dough and place about 1 inch apart on the cookie sheets.

4. Bake for about 15 minutes, or until you can smell a wonderful chocolate aroma filling the air. Transfer to a wire rack and let cool.

Makes about 5 dozen cookies

CHOCOLATE SUGAR COOKIE CUTOUTS

This is a classic cutout sugar cookie with a chocolate flair. You can do just about anything with this dough! If you prefer not to make shapes, you can simply scoop out the dough, press it flat, sprinkle some sugar on it, and bake it. You can also frost the cookies if you like. I use Wilton meringue powder to make royal icing.

★ ★

1¼ cups (2½ sticks) butter, room temperature

1 cup granulated sugar

½ cup firmly packed light brown sugar

1 egg

1 teaspoon baking powder

1 teaspoon salt

1 teaspoon cream of tartar

1 teaspoon vanilla extract

2 tablespoons milk

⅔ cup unsweetened cocoa powder

3 cups all-purpose flour, plus more for rolling

NOTE: There's always some leftover dough when you make cutouts. Gather the dough into teaspoon-size balls, press flat, sprinkle some sugar on them, and bake.

1. Preheat the oven to 350°F/175°C. Line two cookie sheets with parchment paper.

2. Combine the butter, granulated sugar, brown sugar, egg, baking powder, salt, cream of tartar, vanilla, and milk in a large mixing bowl. Mix well, preferably with an electric mixer, occasionally scraping the sides of the bowl. Add the cocoa powder and flour, and mix well.

3. Sprinkle some flour on your work surface and the top of the dough. Roll out the dough to be ⅛ to ¼ inch thick. Use your favorite cookie cutters and cut out your shapes, then place them on the cookie sheets.

4. Bake for about 15 minutes or until they start looking dry. Transfer to a wire rack and let cool.

Makes about 2½ dozen cookies

COLORADO

As rocky as the state itself, this cookie is chock-full of oats, almonds, raisins, and chocolate chips. It's a sensual, but wholesome, treat.

★ ★

1 cup (2 sticks) butter, room temperature

1 cup granulated sugar

1¼ cups firmly packed dark brown sugar

2 eggs

1 teaspoon baking soda

½ teaspoon salt

2 tablespoons molasses

2 teaspoons vanilla extract

2 tablespoons milk

2 cups all-purpose flour

3 cups old-fashioned rolled oats

1 cup raisins

1 cup coarsely chopped almonds

2 cups semisweet chocolate chips

1. Preheat the oven to 375°F/190°C. If you're not using nonstick cookie sheets, line them with parchment paper.

2. Combine the butter, granulated sugar, brown sugar, eggs, baking soda, salt, molasses, vanilla, and milk in a large mixing bowl. Mix well, preferably with an electric mixer, occasionally scraping the sides of the bowl. Add the flour and oats, and mix again. Add the raisins, almonds, and chocolate chips, and mix again until everything is well blended.

3. Using a 1½-inch cookie scoop or a large rounded teaspoon, scoop out the dough and place about 1 inch apart on the cookie sheets.

4. Bake for about 15 minutes, or until the edges look a bit darker. Transfer to a wire rack and let cool.

Makes about 5 dozen cookies

HIT THE TRAILS RUNNING

This cookie is trail mix packed neatly in a cookie, with a little jolt.

* *

1 cup (2 sticks) butter, room temperature

1¼ cups firmly packed light brown sugar

1 cup granulated sugar

2 eggs

1 teaspoon baking soda

1 teaspoon salt

Contents of 1 black tea bag

1 tablespoon vanilla extract

1 tablespoon honey

1 tablespoon pure maple syrup

1 tablespoon milk

3 cups all-purpose flour

3 cups old-fashioned rolled oats

1 cup plain M&M's candies

1 cup peanuts

1 cup semisweet chocolate chips

½ cup raisins

½ cup dried cranberries

¼ cup white chocolate chips

1. Preheat the oven to 350°F/175°C. If you're not using nonstick cookie sheets, line them with parchment paper.

2. Combine the butter, brown sugar, granulated sugar, eggs, baking soda, salt, black tea, vanilla, honey, maple syrup, and milk in a large mixing bowl. Mix well, preferably using an electric mixer, occasionally scraping the sides of the bowl. Add the flour and oats, and mix well. Then add the M&M's, peanuts, semisweet chocolate chips, raisins, dried cranberries, and white chocolate chips. Mix, mix, mix.

3. Using a 1½-inch cookie scoop or a large rounded teaspoon, scoop out the dough and place about 1 inch apart on the cookie sheets.

4. Bake for 15 to 17 minutes, until the edges start to turn golden. Transfer to a wire rack and let cool.

Makes about 4½ dozen cookies

MINT DOUBLE CHOCOLATE CHIP

In the mood for a Girl Scouts' Thin Mint cookie? This is the adult version of the classic.

— ★ ★ —

1 cup (2 sticks) butter, room temperature

1 cup granulated sugar

1/2 cup firmly packed dark brown sugar

2 eggs

1 teaspoon vanilla extract

1 tablespoon mint extract

1/4 teaspoon baking powder

1/4 teaspoon salt

1/2 teaspoon baking soda

2/3 cup Hershey's Special Dark unsweetened cocoa powder

2 cups all-purpose flour

2 cups semisweet chocolate chips

1 cup confectioners' sugar

1. Preheat the oven to 375°F/190°C. If you're not using nonstick cookie sheets, line them with parchment paper.

2. Combine the butter, granulated sugar, brown sugar, eggs, vanilla, mint extract, baking powder, salt, and baking soda in a large mixing bowl. Mix well, preferably with an electric mixer, occasionally scraping the sides of the bowl. Add the cocoa powder, flour, and chocolate chips, and mix well again.

3. Using a 1½-inch cookie scoop or a large rounded teaspoon, scoop out the dough and roll it between the palms of your hands into balls. Roll the balls in the confectioners' sugar, then place about 1 inch apart on the cookie sheets.

4. Bake for 13 to 15 minutes, until you can smell a wonderful chocolate aroma filling the air. Transfer to a wire rack and let cool.

Makes about 3 dozen cookies

NANTUCKET

Ah, Nantucket, how I love thee, with your bold cranberries, your bittersweet chocolate chips, your sea air, and all your hidden treasures.

⋆ ⋆

1 cup (2 sticks) butter, room temperature

1/2 cup vegetable oil

2 eggs

1 cup granulated sugar

1 cup firmly packed light brown sugar

1 tablespoon vanilla extract

1/2 teaspoon almond extract

1 1/2 teaspoons baking powder

1 teaspoon baking soda

1/2 teaspoon sea salt

3 cups all-purpose flour

2 cups bittersweet chocolate chips

1 1/2 cups dried cranberries

1 cup coarsely chopped hazelnuts

1/2 cup semisweet chocolate chips

1. Preheat the oven to 350°F/175°C. If you're not using nonstick cookie sheets, line them with parchment paper.

2. Combine the butter, vegetable oil, eggs, granulated sugar, brown sugar, vanilla, and almond extract in a large mixing bowl. Mix well, preferably with an electric mixer, occasionally scraping the sides of the bowl. Add the baking powder, baking soda, salt, and flour, and mix again. Add the bittersweet chocolate chips, dried cranberries, hazelnuts, and semisweet chocolate chips, and mix one more time until all the ingredients are well combined.

3. Using a 1½-inch cookie scoop or a larger rounded tablespoon, scoop out the dough and place about 1½ inches apart on the cookie sheets.

4. Bake for about 20 minutes, or until the edges are golden brown. Transfer to a wire rack and let cool.

Makes about 4 dozen cookies

PECAN CHOCOLATE SHORTY

A pecan butter ball meets a shortbread cookie, plus a little chocolate, because who doesn't like chocolate?

* *

1½ cups (3 sticks) butter, room temperature

1 cup granulated sugar

¾ cup firmly packed light brown sugar

1 egg

1 teaspoon baking powder

1 teaspoon salt

1 tablespoon vanilla extract

3 cups all-purpose flour

1 cup chopped pecans

1½ cups semisweet chocolate chips

1. Preheat the oven to 365°F/185°C. If you're not using nonstick cookie sheets, line them with parchment paper.

2. Combine the butter, granulated sugar, brown sugar, egg, baking powder, salt, and vanilla in a large mixing bowl. Mix well, preferably with an electric mixer, occasionally scraping the sides of the bowl. Add the flour, mix well, then add the pecans and chocolate chips, and mix until everything is well blended.

3. Using a 1-inch cookie scoop or a rounded teaspoon, scoop out the dough and drop about 1 inch apart on the cookie sheets. Flatten the rounded balls by pressing down with the back of a spatula.

4. Bake for about 15 minutes, or until the edges are golden brown. Transfer to a wire rack and let cool.

Makes about 5 dozen cookies

WINTER IN THE BERKSHIRES

This cookie makes me think of standing outside in the middle of
winter with a candy cane in my cup of hot chocolate.

* *

1¼ cups (2½ sticks) butter, room temperature

4 candy canes, broken into bits, or ¼ cup peppermint stick bits

1½ cups firmly packed light brown sugar

2 eggs

2 teaspoons baking powder

½ teaspoon salt

1 tablespoon peppermint extract

2 tablespoons milk

⅔ cup Hershey's Special Dark unsweetened cocoa powder

2 cups all-purpose flour

½ cup white chocolate chips

2 cups semisweet chocolate chips

1. Preheat the oven to 350°F/175°C. Line one cookie sheet with parchment paper.

2. Combine the butter and peppermint candy in a large mixing bowl and beat, preferably with an electric mixer. Add the brown sugar, eggs, baking powder, salt, and peppermint extract. Mix well, occasionally scraping the sides of the bowl. Add the milk, cocoa powder, flour, white chocolate chips, and semisweet chocolate chips, and mix until well combined.

3. Using a 1-inch cookie scoop or a rounded teaspoon, scoop out the dough and drop 1 inch apart on the parchment-lined cookie sheet.

4. Bake for 15 to 17 minutes, until you can smell a wonderful chocolate aroma filling the air. Let cool on the cookie sheet for 5 to 10 minutes, then transfer to a wire rack and let cool fully.

Makes about 3 dozen cookies

APPLES ROLLED IN AUTUMN

If you love apple crisp, you will love this cookie. With its apples, oats, brown sugar, cinnamon, nutmeg, and walnuts, it's practically the same thing in cookie form. My brother likes to heat up a few cookies in a bowl and put vanilla ice cream on top of them.

* *

1 cup (2 sticks) butter, room temperature

2 egg yolks

1 medium apple (any variety), peeled and chopped

1 cup granulated sugar

1 cup firmly packed light brown sugar

3 teaspoons ground cinnamon

1/2 teaspoon salt

1/4 teaspoon ground nutmeg

2 teaspoons baking powder

1 tablespoon vanilla extract

1 cup old-fashioned rolled oats

3 cups all-purpose flour

1 cup chopped walnuts

1. Preheat the oven to 335°F/170°C. If you're not using nonstick cookie sheets, line them with parchment paper.

2. Combine the butter, egg yolks, apple, granulated sugar, brown sugar, cinnamon, salt, nutmeg, baking powder, and vanilla in a large mixing bowl. Mix well, preferably with an electric mixer, occasionally scraping the sides of the bowl. Beat in the oats and flour until well combined, then mix in the walnuts.

3. Using a 1-inch cookie scoop or a rounded teaspoon, scoop out the dough and drop about 1 inch apart on the cookie sheets.

4. Bake for 20 to 25 minutes, until the edges are slightly brown. Transfer to a wire rack and let cool.

Makes about 4 dozen cookies

CHUKIE'S PECAN DREAM

When I was growing up, my mother always put a similar cookie in the lunch bag for my dad, Chukie. He loved the crunch of the cookie and the heartiness of the pecans and butter. Who doesn't love butter?

* *

2 cups (4 sticks) butter, room temperature

1 cup granulated sugar

1/2 cup firmly packed light brown sugar

1/2 teaspoon salt

2 teaspoons cream of tartar

1 teaspoon ground cinnamon

2 teaspoons vanilla extract

1 egg yolk

1 teaspoon almond extract

4 cups all-purpose flour

2 cups chopped pecans

1. Preheat the oven to 355°F/180°C. If you're not using nonstick cookie sheets, line them with parchment paper.

2. Combine the butter, granulated sugar, brown sugar, salt, cream of tartar, cinnamon, vanilla, egg yolk, and almond extract in a large mixing bowl. Mix well, preferably with an electric mixer, occasionally scraping the sides of the bowl. Add the flour and mix well, then add the pecans and mix until everything is well blended.

3. Using a 1-inch cookie scoop or a rounded teaspoon, scoop out the dough and drop about 1 inch apart on the cookie sheets. Flatten the rounded dough with the back of a spatula.

4. Bake for about 18 minutes, or until the edges are golden. Transfer to a wire rack and let cool.

Makes about 5 dozen cookies

KEY LIME

Ahh, I feel like I'm back in Key West with the sun on my face, a warm breeze, and the smell of crisp, fresh lime.

* *

½ cup (1 stick) butter, room temperature

½ cup vegetable oil

1 cup granulated sugar

1 tablespoon vanilla extract

1 tablespoon lime extract

1 teaspoon baking powder

1 teaspoon baking soda

½ teaspoon salt

1 egg

3 cups all-purpose flour

FROSTING

1 cup confectioners' sugar

3 tablespoons milk

½ teaspoon lime extract

1. Preheat the oven to 365°F/185°C. If you're not using nonstick cookie sheets, line them with parchment paper.

2. Combine the butter, vegetable oil, granulated sugar, vanilla, lime extract, baking powder, baking soda, salt, and egg in a large mixing bowl. Mix well, preferably with an electric mixer, occasionally scraping the sides of the bowl. Add the flour and mix well.

3. Using a 1-inch cookie scoop or a rounded teaspoon, scoop out the dough and drop 1 inch apart on the cookie sheets. Flatten the rounded dough with the back of a spatula.

4. Bake for 14 to 17 minutes, until the edges are slightly golden. Transfer to a wire rack and let cool. I usually then place the cookies in a lidded storage container and put them in the freezer or a cool place until I am ready to frost them.

5. When you are ready to frost the cookies, combine the confectioners' sugar, milk, and lime extract in a medium mixing bowl. Mix until the frosting has a loose paste-like consistency. Using a fork or whisk, drizzle lines of frosting over the cookies.

Makes about 3½ dozen cookies

LEMON CHERRY

This sweet, crisp, light cookie is full of mild lemon flavor
with a hint of tart cherries.

1/2 cup (1 stick) butter, room
temperature

1/2 cup vegetable oil

1 cup sugar

2 eggs

1 tablespoon lemon extract

1 teaspoon baking powder

1 teaspoon baking soda

1/2 teaspoon salt

1 1/2 cups dried tart cherries

3 cups all-purpose flour

1. Preheat the oven to 370°F/188°C. If
   you're not using nonstick cookie sheets,
   line them with parchment paper.

2. Combine the butter, vegetable oil, sugar, eggs,
   lemon extract, baking powder, baking soda,
   and salt in a large mixing bowl. Mix well, preferably with an electric mixer, occasionally
   scraping the sides of the bowl. Add the dried
   cherries and mix well, then add the flour and
   mix until well blended.

3. Using a 1 1/2-inch cookie scoop or a rounded
   teaspoon, scoop out the dough and place about
   1 inch apart on the cookie sheets.

4. Bake for 15 to 17 minutes, until the edges are
   golden. Transfer to a wire rack and let cool.

Makes about 3 1/2 dozen cookies

LEMON GINGER

The combination of lemon and ginger in this cookie will make your tongue tingle!

* *

1 cup (2 sticks) butter, room temperature

1 cup sugar

2 eggs

2 tablespoons vanilla yogurt

2 teaspoons lemon extract

3 teaspoons ground ginger

1 teaspoon baking soda

1 teaspoon cream of tartar

1 teaspoon baking powder

1/2 teaspoon salt

3 cups all-purpose flour

NOTE: If you love ginger and want this cookie to have more of a ginger flavor, combine 1 tablespoon ground ginger and 2 tablespoons granulated sugar in a bowl. Roll your cookies through the ginger-sugar mixture before baking.

1. Preheat the oven to 355°F/180°C. If you're not using nonstick cookie sheets, line them with parchment paper.

2. Combine the butter, sugar, eggs, yogurt, lemon extract, ginger, baking soda, cream of tartar, baking powder, and salt in a large mixing bowl. Mix well, preferably with an electric mixer, occasionally scraping the sides of the bowl. Add the flour and mix until well blended.

3. Using a 1-inch cookie scoop or a rounded teaspoon, scoop out the dough and place about 1 inch apart on the cookie sheets.

4. Bake for 15 to 17 minutes, until the edges are golden brown. Transfer to a wire rack and let cool.

Makes about 3½ dozen cookies

MACADAMIA NUT

These delightful cookies are sweet but not too sweet. Filled with Hawaiian macadamia nuts and white chocolate chips, they satisfy without weighing you down.

1 cup (2 sticks) butter, room temperature

3/4 cup firmly packed light brown sugar

3/4 cup granulated sugar

2 eggs

1 tablespoon honey

2 teaspoons vanilla extract

1 teaspoon baking soda

1/2 teaspoon baking powder

1/2 teaspoon salt

2 1/2 cups all-purpose flour

1 cup chopped macadamia nuts

1 cup white chocolate chips

1. Preheat the oven to 350°F/175°C. If you're not using nonstick cookie sheets, line them with parchment paper.

2. Combine the butter, brown sugar, granulated sugar, eggs, honey, vanilla, baking soda, baking powder, and salt in a large mixing bowl. Mix well, preferably with an electric mixer, occasionally scraping the sides of the bowl. Add the flour and mix again, then add the macadamia nuts and white chocolate chips, and mix well.

3. Using a 1½-inch cookie scoop or a large rounded teaspoon, scoop out the dough and place about 1 inch apart on the cookie sheets.

4. Bake for 15 to 17 minutes, until the edges are golden. Transfer to a wire rack and let cool.

Makes about 4½ dozen cookies

NINA'S CUP OF TEA

Sweet, just like Nina herself, this little almond cookie is perfect with a cup of tea.

* *

1¼ cups (2½ sticks) butter, room temperature

1 cup granulated sugar

½ cup firmly packed light brown sugar

2 eggs

½ teaspoon salt

1 teaspoon cream of tartar

1 teaspoon baking powder

2 teaspoons almond extract

2 teaspoons vanilla extract

2 tablespoons pure maple syrup

2 tablespoons milk

3½ cups all-purpose flour

1 cup slivered or sliced almonds

1. Preheat the oven to 350°F/175°C. If you're not using nonstick cookie sheets, line them with parchment paper.

2. Combine the butter, granulated sugar, brown sugar, eggs, salt, cream of tartar, baking powder, almond extract, vanilla, maple syrup, and milk in a large mixing bowl. Mix well, preferably with an electric mixer, occasionally scraping the sides of the bowl. Add the flour and almonds, and mix well once more.

3. Using a 1-inch cookie scoop or a rounded teaspoon, scoop out the dough and drop 1 inch apart on the cookie sheets.

4. Bake for 15 to 18 minutes, until the edges are slightly golden. Transfer to a wire rack and let cool.

Makes about 5 dozen cookies

ORANGE CREAM

Like orange Creamsicles? This is a mild cookie version of the delectable frozen treat.

* *

1¹/₂ cups (3 sticks) butter, room temperature

1¹/₂ cups sugar

4 eggs

1 teaspoon vanilla extract

1 tablespoon orange extract

2 teaspoons baking powder

1 teaspoon cream of tartar

2 tablespoons orange zest

¹/₄ cup orange juice

4 cups all-purpose flour

1 cup white chocolate chips

1. Preheat the oven to 355°F/180°C. If you're not using nonstick cookie sheets, line them with parchment paper.

2. Combine the butter, sugar, eggs, vanilla, orange extract, baking powder, cream of tartar, and orange zest in a large mixing bowl. Mix well, preferably with an electric mixer, occasionally scraping the sides of the bowl. Add the orange juice and mix well, then add the flour and white chocolate chips, and mix well again.

3. Using a 1-inch cookie scoop or a rounded teaspoon, scoop out the dough and drop about 1 inch apart on the cookie sheets.

4. Bake for about 15 minutes, or until the edges are golden brown. Transfer to a wire rack and let cool.

Makes about 5 dozen cookies

PECAN BUTTER BALLS

These fancy little snowballs usually come out around the holidays.
With their hearty pecans and fluffy sweetness, no one can pass
them up. I dare you to try them in the summer!

* *

1¼ cups (2½ sticks) butter, room
    temperature

½ cup granulated sugar

1 teaspoon ground cinnamon

1 teaspoon vanilla extract

½ teaspoon lemon juice

1 tablespoon honey

2 cups all-purpose flour

2 cups chopped pecans

1 cup confectioners' sugar

1. Preheat the oven to 325°F/160°C. If
   you're not using nonstick cookie sheets,
   line them with parchment paper.

2. Combine the butter, granulated sugar, cinnamon, vanilla, lemon juice, and honey in a large
   mixing bowl. Mix well, preferably with an electric mixer, occasionally scraping the sides of the
   bowl. Add the flour and pecans, and mix well.

3. Using a 1-inch scoop or a rounded teaspoon,
   scoop out the dough, roll it between the palms
   of your hands into balls, and drop about ½ inch
   apart on the cookie sheets.

4. Bake for about 30 minutes, or until the edges
   are golden. Transfer to a wire rack and let cool
   slightly.

5. Pour the confectioners' sugar into a long, flat
   container. Roll the warm cookies in the sugar,
   let cool, then roll in the sugar again.

Makes about 3½ dozen cookies

RUM RAISIN

Remember rum raisin ice cream? Here it is in a cookie, and it won't melt in the sun!

* *

1 cup (2 sticks) butter, room temperature

3/4 cup firmly packed dark brown sugar

1/2 cup granulated sugar

2 eggs

1 teaspoon baking powder

1/2 teaspoon baking soda

1/2 teaspoon salt

1 tablespoon pure maple syrup

1 generous tablespoon plus 1 teaspoon rum extract

2 1/2 cups all-purpose flour

1 1/2 cups Raisinets (an 11-ounce package)

1. Preheat the oven to 360°F/180°C. If you're not using nonstick cookie sheets, line them with parchment paper.

2. Combine the butter, brown sugar, granulated sugar, eggs, baking powder, baking soda, salt, maple syrup, and rum extract in a large mixing bowl. Mix well, preferably with an electric mixer, occasionally scraping the sides of the bowl. Add the flour and mix well, then add the Raisinets and mix again.

3. Using a 1½-inch cookie scoop or a large rounded teaspoon, scoop out the dough and place about 1 inch apart on the cookie sheets.

4. Bake for about 18 minutes, or until the edges are golden brown. Transfer to a wire rack and let cool.

Makes about 3½ dozen cookies

VANILLA WALNUT PEAR

This delicious fall treat is full of spices, mild pear, and walnuts. It's great for brunch or paired with some vanilla ice cream.

* *

1 cup (2 sticks) butter, room temperature

1 cup granulated sugar

1/2 cup firmly packed light brown sugar

2 egg yolks

1/2 teaspoon salt

1/4 teaspoon ground nutmeg

1 teaspoon ground cinnamon

2 tablespoons vanilla extract

1 teaspoon baking powder

3 cups all-purpose flour

1 cup chopped walnuts

1 medium pear, peeled and chopped

1. Preheat the oven to 355°F/180°C. If you're not using nonstick cookie sheets, line them with parchment paper.

2. Combine the butter, granulated sugar, brown sugar, egg yolks, salt, nutmeg, cinnamon, vanilla, and baking powder in a large mixing bowl. Mix well, preferably with an electric mixer, until everything is combined, occasionally scraping the sides of the bowl. Beat in the flour; mix in the walnuts and pear.

3. Using a 1-inch cookie scoop or a rounded teaspoon, scoop out the dough and drop about 1½ inches apart on the cookie sheets.

4. Bake for about 20 minutes, or until the edges are slightly golden brown. Transfer to a wire rack and let cool.

Makes about 3 dozen cookies

BRANDI ALEXANDER

This cookie packs all the flavor of a Brandy Alexander cocktail without all the buzz. Instead you will be left with a warm, fuzzy feeling.

— ⋆ ⋆ —

1¼ cups (2½ sticks) butter, room temperature

1 cup firmly packed light brown sugar

½ cup granulated sugar

2 eggs

1 teaspoon baking soda

1 teaspoon cream of tartar

½ teaspoon salt

1 tablespoon crème de cacao

1 tablespoon brandy extract

¼ teaspoon ground nutmeg

2¾ cups all-purpose flour

¾ cup white chocolate chips

1. Preheat the oven to 350°F/175°C. If you're not using nonstick cookie sheets, line them with parchment paper.

2. Combine the butter, brown sugar, granulated sugar, eggs, baking soda, cream of tartar, salt, crème de cacao, brandy extract, and nutmeg in a large mixing bowl. Mix well, preferably with an electric mixer, occasionally scraping the sides of the bowl. Add the flour and white chocolate chips, and mix until everything is well blended.

3. Using a 1-inch cookie scoop or a rounded teaspoon, scoop out the dough and place about 1 inch apart on the cookie sheets.

4. Bake for about 16 minutes, or until the edges are golden brown. Transfer to a wire rack and let cool.

Makes about 3½ dozen cookies

CINNAMON MORNING

Looking for a breakfast cookie you won't feel guilty about?
This is your cookie. If you want to make these cookies a little
fancier, roll the dough in a cinnamon-sugar combination
(1 tablespoon cinnamon, 2 tablespoons granulated sugar).

— ★ ★ —

1½ cups (3 sticks) butter, room temperature

1 cup granulated sugar

½ cup firmly packed light brown sugar

1 egg

½ teaspoon salt

1 teaspoon ground cinnamon

1 teaspoon cream of tartar

1 teaspoon vanilla extract

3 cups all-purpose flour

1 (10-ounce) bag Hershey's cinnamon chips

1. Preheat the oven to 360°F/180°C. If you're not using nonstick cookie sheets, line them with parchment paper.

2. Combine the butter, granulated sugar, brown sugar, egg, salt, cinnamon, cream of tartar, and vanilla in a large mixing bowl. Mix well, preferably with an electric mixer, occasionally scraping the sides of the bowl. Add the flour and mix well, then add the cinnamon chips and mix until everything is well blended.

3. Using a 1-inch cookie scoop or a rounded teaspoon, scoop out the dough and place about 1 inch apart on the cookie sheets.

4. Bake for 15 to 17 minutes, until the edges are slightly golden. Transfer to a wire rack and let cool.

Makes about 3½ dozen cookies

ITALIAN WEDDING

Ever been to a wedding and at the end of the night, much to your surprise, you're served homemade Italian cookies made by the grandmother of the bride or groom? Well, here's that cookie!

— * * —

1 cup (2 sticks) butter, room temperature

1 cup granulated sugar

5 eggs

1 teaspoon vanilla extract

1 teaspoon lemon extract

1 teaspoon orange extract

1 teaspoon anise extract

4 teaspoons baking powder

4 cups all-purpose flour

FROSTING

1½ cups confectioners' sugar

¼ cup milk

1 teaspoon lemon extract

Multicolored sprinkles (I use nonpareils)

1. Preheat the oven to 350°F/175°C. If you're not using nonstick cookie sheets, line them with parchment paper.

2. Combine the butter, granulated sugar, eggs, vanilla, lemon extract, orange extract, anise extract, and baking powder in a large mixing bowl. Mix well, preferably with an electric mixer, occasionally scraping the sides of the bowl. Add the flour and mix well.

3. Using a 1-inch cookie scoop or a rounded teaspoon, scoop out the dough and place about ½ inch apart on the cookie sheets.

4. Bake for 12 to 15 minutes, or until the edges are golden. Transfer to a wire rack and let cool. I usually then place the cookies in a lidded storage container and put them in the freezer or a cool place until I am ready to frost them.

5. When you are ready to frost the cookies, combine the confectioners' sugar, milk, and lemon extract in a medium mixing bowl. Mix until you get a loose paste-like consistency.

6. Using the back of a small spoon (I use one of my daughter's old baby spoons), spread the frosting on the cookies. Dip the freshly frosted cookies into a bowl of sprinkles.

Makes about 4½ dozen cookies

PUMPKIN SPICE

Here it is fall again, with pumpkins at roadside farm stands and spices filling the air.

★ ★

½ cup (1 stick) butter, room temperature

1 cup granulated sugar

½ cup firmly packed dark brown sugar

½ cup canned pumpkin purée

1 egg

1 tablespoon vanilla extract

1 tablespoon molasses

2 teaspoons ground cinnamon

¼ teaspoon ground nutmeg

½ teaspoon salt

1 teaspoon baking soda

1 teaspoon baking powder

3 cups all-purpose flour

1. Preheat the oven to 350°F/175°C. If you're not using nonstick cookie sheets, line them with parchment paper.

2. Combine the butter, granulated sugar, brown sugar, pumpkin purée, egg, vanilla, molasses, cinnamon, nutmeg, salt, baking soda, and baking powder in a large mixing bowl. Mix well, preferably with an electric mixer, occasionally scraping the sides of the bowl. Add the flour and mix until well blended.

3. Using a 1-inch cookie scoop or a rounded teaspoon, scoop out the dough and place about 1 inch apart on the cookie sheets.

4. Bake for about 18 minutes, or until the edges are darker in color. Transfer to a wire rack and let cool.

Makes about 5 dozen cookies

THE VERMONT

This chewy cookie is filled with all the rich maple flavor you would expect from a cookie called Vermont. If you're like my brother and feel a little nutty, walnuts are a nice addition.

— ★ ★ —

1 cup (2 sticks) butter, room temperature

1½ cups firmly packed brown sugar

1 egg

2 teaspoons baking powder

½ teaspoon salt

1 tablespoon maple extract

1 tablespoon pure maple syrup

2½ cups all-purpose flour

1 cup chopped walnuts (optional)

1. Preheat the oven to 360°F/180°C. If you're not using nonstick cookie sheets, line them with parchment paper.

2. Combine the butter, brown sugar, egg, baking powder, salt, maple extract, and maple syrup in a large mixing bowl. Mix well, preferably with an electric mixer, occasionally scraping the sides of the bowl. Add the flour and mix until well blended. Add the walnuts, if using, and mix again until well blended.

3. Using a 1-inch cookie scoop or a rounded teaspoon, scoop out the dough and place about 1 inch apart on the cookie sheets.

4. Bake for 15 to 17 minutes, until the edges are darker in color. Transfer to a wire rack and let cool.

Makes about 3½ dozen cookies

CHEWY CHOCOLATE CHIP

Melt back into your childhood. This cookie is warm and cozy, and it makes time stand still.

1¼ cups (2½ sticks) butter, room temperature

2 cups firmly packed light brown sugar

3 eggs

1 teaspoon salt

1 teaspoon baking soda

1 teaspoon baking powder

1 tablespoon vanilla extract

3½ cups all-purpose flour

2 cups semisweet chocolate chips

NOTE: Want a more festive cookie? Add ½ cup of your favorite colorful sprinkles when you add the chocolate chips.

NOTE: Want shapes or bars? Spread out your dough about ¾ inch thick on a nonstick cookie sheet. Bake for 20 to 25 minutes, until the edges are golden brown, then let the dough cool on the cookie sheet for about 10 minutes. Turn the cookie sheet over onto a wire rack, then flip onto a large cutting board and cut into bars using a knife or into shapes using a cookie cutter.

1. Preheat the oven to 330°F/165°C. If you're not using nonstick cookie sheets, line them with parchment paper.

2. Combine the butter, brown sugar, eggs, salt, baking soda, baking powder, and vanilla in a large mixing bowl. Mix well, preferably with an electric mixer, occasionally scraping the sides of the bowl. Add the flour and mix until well combined, then add the chocolate chips and mix again.

3. Using a 1-inch cookie scoop or a rounded teaspoon, scoop out the dough and place about 1 inch apart on the cookie sheets.

4. Bake for 18 to 20 minutes, until the edges are golden brown. Transfer to a wire rack and let cool.

Makes about 4 dozen cookies

GINGER MOLASSES

This cookie is good at any time of the year. With its warm ginger and other spices, it pairs well with a glass of milk and is even better served warm in the winter.

1 cup (2 sticks) butter, room temperature

1 cup granulated sugar

1/2 cup firmly packed dark brown sugar

1 egg

1/4 cup molasses

1 teaspoon baking soda

1 teaspoon baking powder

1/2 teaspoon salt

1 teaspoon ground cinnamon

1 teaspoon ground ginger

2 1/2 cups all-purpose flour

1. Preheat the oven to 375°F/190°C. If you're not using nonstick cookie sheets, line them with parchment paper.

2. Combine the butter, granulated sugar, brown sugar, egg, molasses, baking soda, baking powder, salt, cinnamon, and ginger in a large mixing bowl. Mix well, preferably with an electric mixer, occasionally scraping the sides of the bowl. Add the flour and mix until well blended.

3. Using a 1-inch cookie scoop or a rounded teaspoon, scoop out the dough and place about 1 inch apart on the cookie sheets.

4. Bake for about 15 minutes, or until the edges are darker in color. Transfer to a wire rack and let cool.

Makes about 3 dozen cookies

KISS ME

What to eat first? The chocolate Hershey's Kiss or the peanut butter bottom? This is my auntie's classic Hershey's Kiss cookie.

½ cup (1 stick) butter, room temperature

1 cup creamy peanut butter

½ cup vegetable oil

1 cup firmly packed light brown sugar

1½ cups granulated sugar

2 eggs

3 tablespoons half-and-half

1 teaspoon vanilla extract

1 tablespoon honey

1 teaspoon baking powder

1 teaspoon baking soda

2½ cups all-purpose flour

1 (12-ounce) bag Hershey's Kisses

1. Preheat the oven to 355°F/180°C. If you're not using nonstick cookie sheets, line them with parchment paper.

2. Combine the butter, peanut butter, vegetable oil, brown sugar, ½ cup of the granulated sugar, eggs, half-and-half, vanilla, honey, baking powder, and baking soda in a large mixing bowl. Mix well, preferably with an electric mixer, occasionally scraping the sides of the bowl. Add the flour and mix well, scraping the sides of the bowl.

3. Place the remaining 1 cup granulated sugar in a medium bowl or shallow container. Shape the dough into 1-inch balls and roll the balls through the sugar. Place the balls about 1 inch apart on the cookie sheets.

4. Bake for 12 to 15 minutes, until the edges are lightly golden. (While the cookies bake, unwrap the Hershey's Kisses.) Immediately push a Kiss into the top of each cookie, then transfer to a wire rack and let cool.

Makes about 4½ dozen cookies

LUCILLE'S PEANUT BUTTER

My grandmother Lucille made the best peanut butter cookies.
I especially loved the marks she made with the fork tines.
These cookies are full of rich peanut buttery flavor and have
that extra-special look.

½ cup (1 stick) butter, room temperature

½ cup vegetable oil

1 cup crunchy peanut butter

1 cup granulated sugar

1 cup firmly packed light brown sugar

3 eggs

½ teaspoon salt

1 teaspoon baking powder

1 teaspoon baking soda

1 tablespoon honey

2 teaspoons vanilla extract

3 cups all-purpose flour

1. Preheat the oven to 350°F/175°C. If you're not using nonstick cookie sheets, line them with parchment paper.

2. Combine the butter, vegetable oil, peanut butter, granulated sugar, brown sugar, eggs, salt, baking powder, baking soda, honey, and vanilla in a large mixing bowl. Mix well, preferably with an electric mixer, occasionally scraping the sides of the bowl. Add the flour and mix until well blended.

3. Using a 1-inch cookie scoop or a rounded teaspoon, scoop out the dough and place about 1 inch apart on the cookie sheets. Using a fork, make a crisscross pattern in each ball of dough.

4. Bake for about 15 minutes, or until the edges are golden brown. Transfer to a wire rack and let cool.

Makes about 5 dozen cookies

NONI'S OLD-FASHIONED SPICE RAISIN

This cookie is as spicy as my Noni was. With all of its cinnamon, nutmeg, and molasses, it will tantalize your tongue.

1 cup (2 sticks) butter, room temperature

1 cup granulated sugar

1 cup firmly packed dark brown sugar

2 eggs

1 tablespoon vanilla extract

1 teaspoon baking soda

1 teaspoon baking powder

1 teaspoon salt

1½ teaspoons ground cinnamon

½ teaspoon ground nutmeg

1 tablespoon molasses

3 cups all-purpose flour

2 cups raisins

NOTE: Just for fun, you could use 1 cup dark raisins and 1 cup golden raisins.

1. Preheat the oven to 325°F/160°C. If you're not using nonstick cookie sheets, line them with parchment paper.

2. Combine the butter, granulated sugar, brown sugar, eggs, vanilla, baking soda, baking powder, salt, cinnamon, nutmeg, and molasses in a large mixing bowl. Mix well, preferably with an electric mixer, occasionally scraping the sides of the bowl. Add the flour and mix until well blended. Add the raisins and mix until well combined.

3. Using a 1-inch cookie scoop or a rounded teaspoon, scoop out the dough and place about 1 inch apart on the cookie sheets.

4. Bake for 18 to 20 minutes, until the edges are golden brown. Transfer to a wire rack and let cool.

Makes about 5 dozen cookies

OATMEAL RAISIN

This cookie is reminiscent of days gone by. It doesn't get much
more classic than this.

1 cup (2 sticks) butter, room
temperature

1 cup granulated sugar

1 cup firmly packed light brown
sugar

2 eggs

1 teaspoon vanilla extract

1 teaspoon baking soda

1/2 teaspoon baking powder

1 teaspoon salt

1 teaspoon ground cinnamon

1/4 teaspoon ground nutmeg

1 tablespoon pure maple syrup

3 cups old-fashioned rolled oats

2 cups all-purpose flour

1 1/2 cups raisins

1. Preheat the oven to 365°F/185°C. If
   you're not using nonstick cookie sheets,
   line them with parchment paper.

2. Combine the butter, granulated sugar, brown
   sugar, eggs, vanilla, baking soda, baking powder, salt, cinnamon, nutmeg, and maple syrup
   in a large mixing bowl. Mix well, preferably
   with an electric mixer, occasionally scraping
   the sides of the bowl. Add the oats and mix
   well, then add the flour and mix well again. Add
   the raisins and mix until well combined. Scrape
   the sides of the bowl as needed.

3. Using a 1½-inch cookie scoop or a large
   rounded teaspoon, scoop out the dough and
   place about 1½ inches apart on the cookie
   sheets.

4. Bake for about 15 minutes, or until the edges
   are golden brown. Transfer to a wire rack and
   let cool.

Makes about 4½ dozen cookies

OUT-OF-THIS-WORLD CHOCOLATE CHIP

This is not your grandma's chocolate chip cookie. This cookie packs a punch! With hills and valleys of white and semisweet chocolate chips, walnuts, and a bite of sea salt, it will keep you coming back for more.

1¼ cups (2½ sticks) butter, room temperature

1½ cups firmly packed light brown sugar

1 cup granulated sugar

2 eggs

1 teaspoon coarse sea salt

1½ teaspoons baking soda

1½ teaspoons baking powder

1 tablespoon vanilla extract

3½ cups all-purpose flour

2 cups semisweet chocolate chips

½ cup white chocolate chips

1 cup chopped walnuts

NOTE: Want shapes or bars? Spread the dough about ¾ inch thick on a nonstick cookie sheet. Bake for 20 to 25 minutes, until the edges are golden brown. Let cool for about 10 minutes before turning onto a cutting board and cutting into shapes or bars.

1. Preheat the oven to 350°F/175°C. If you're not using nonstick cookie sheets, line them with parchment paper.

2. Combine the butter, brown sugar, granulated sugar, eggs, salt, baking soda, baking powder, and vanilla in a large mixing bowl. Mix well, preferably with an electric mixer, occasionally scraping the sides of the bowl. Add the flour and mix, then add the semisweet chocolate chips, white chocolate chips, and walnuts, and mix well again.

3. Using a 1½-inch cookie scoop or a large rounded teaspoon, scoop out the dough and place about 1 inch apart on the cookie sheets.

4. Bake for 15 to 17 minutes, or until golden. Transfer to a wire rack and let cool.

Makes about 4 dozen cookies

SHORTBREAD

This simple, tasty cookie has brought tears to a grown woman's eyes. It will bring you back to your grandma's house, when you were little, and will be a tradition for years to come.

* * *

2 cups (4 sticks) butter, room temperature

1 cup sugar

½ teaspoon salt

1 teaspoon cream of tartar

2 teaspoons vanilla extract

4 cups all-purpose flour

1. Preheat the oven to 350°F/175°C. If you're not using nonstick cookie sheets, line them with parchment paper.

2. Combine the butter, sugar, salt, cream of tartar, and vanilla in a large mixing bowl. Mix well, preferably with an electric mixer, occasionally scraping the sides of the bowl. Add the flour and mix well again.

3. Using a 1-inch cookie scoop or a rounded teaspoon, scoop out the dough and place 1 inch apart on the cookie sheets. Flatten the rounded dough by pressing down with the back of a spatula.

4. Bake for 14 to 17 minutes, or until the edges are slightly golden. Transfer to a wire rack and let cool.

Makes about 4½ dozen cookies

SNICKERDOODLE

Snickerdoodles have been around since the 1800s. They're chewy
yet crisp cookies with a little cinnamon to linger on your lips.

1 cup (2 sticks) butter, room
    temperature

1 1/2 cups plus 2 tablespoons sugar

2 eggs

1 teaspoon baking soda

1 teaspoon cream of tartar

1/2 teaspoon salt

1/8 teaspoon ground nutmeg

3 cups all-purpose flour

1 tablespoon ground cinnamon

1. Preheat the oven to 350°F/175°C. If you're not
using nonstick cookie sheets, line them with
parchment paper.

2. Combine the butter, 1½ cups of the sugar, eggs,
baking soda, cream of tartar, salt, and nutmeg
in a large mixing bowl. Mix well, preferably
with an electric mixer, occasionally scraping
the sides of the bowl. Add the flour and mix
well again.

3. Combine the cinnamon and the remaining
2 tablespoons sugar in a shallow bowl.

4. Using a 1-inch cookie scoop or a rounded teaspoon, scoop out the dough and roll it between
the palms of your hands into balls. Roll the
balls in the cinnamon-sugar mixture. Place
about 1½ inches apart on the cookie sheets.

5. Bake for 12 to 15 minutes, or until the edges are
lightly golden brown. Transfer to a wire rack
and let cool.

Makes about 3 dozen cookies

SUGAR COOKIE CUTOUTS

This is a simple, classic sugar cookie. If you don't want to make shapes, you can drop spoonfuls of dough on a cookie sheet, press them flat, then bake them. If you're looking to frost them, you can use meringue powder to make royal icing.

1 cup (2 sticks) butter, room temperature

1½ cups sugar

1 teaspoon salt

1 teaspoon cream of tartar

1 egg

1 teaspoon lemon juice

1 teaspoon vanilla extract

3 cups all-purpose flour, plus more for rolling

NOTE: There's always some leftover dough when you make cutouts. Gather the dough into teaspoon-size balls, rolling them between the palms of your hands. Press the balls flat with the back of a spatula, sprinkle some sugar on them, and bake.

1. Preheat the oven to 350°F/175°C. Line two cookie sheets with parchment paper.

2. Combine the butter, sugar, salt, cream of tartar, egg, lemon juice, and vanilla in a large mixing bowl. Mix well, preferably with an electric mixer, occasionally scraping the sides of the bowl. Add the flour and mix well again.

3. Sprinkle some flour on your work surface and the top of the dough. Roll out the dough to be ⅛ to ¼ inch thick. Use your favorite cookie cutters to cut out your shapes, then place them on the cookie sheets.

4. Bake for 17 to 20 minutes, or until the edges are slightly golden. Transfer to a wire rack and let cool.

Makes about 3 dozen cookies

METRIC CONVERSION CHARTS

Unless you have finely calibrated measuring equipment, conversions between U.S. and metric measurements will be inexact. It's important to convert the measurements for all the ingredients in a recipe to maintain the same proportions as the original.

GENERAL FORMULA FOR METRIC CONVERSION

Ounces to grams	multiply ounces by 28.35
Grams to ounces	multiply grams by 0.035
Pounds to grams	multiply pounds by 453.5
Pounds to kilograms	multiply pounds by 0.45
Cups to liters	multiply cups by 0.24
Fahrenheit to Celsius	subtract 32 from Fahrenheit temperature, multiply by 5, then divide by 9
Celsius to Fahrenheit	multiply Celsius temperature by 9, divide by 5, then add 32

APPROXIMATE METRIC EQUIVALENTS BY VOLUME

U.S.	Metric
1 teaspoon	5 milliliters
1 tablespoon	15 milliliters
⅓ cup	60 milliliters
½ cup	120 milliliters
1 cup	230 milliliters
1¼ cups	300 milliliters
1½ cups	360 milliliters
2 cups	460 milliliters
2½ cups	600 milliliters
3 cups	700 milliliters
4 cups (1 quart)	0.95 liter
1.06 quarts	1 liter
4 quarts (1 gallon)	3.8 liters

APPROXIMATE METRIC EQUIVALENTS BY WEIGHT

U.S.	Metric	Metric	U.S.
¼ ounce	7 grams	1 gram	0.035 ounce
½ ounce	14 grams	50 grams	1.75 ounces
1 ounce	28 grams	100 grams	3.5 ounces
1¼ ounces	35 grams	250 grams	8.75 ounces
1½ ounces	40 grams	500 grams	1.1 pounds
2½ ounces	70 grams	1 kilogram	2.2 pounds
4 ounces	112 grams		
5 ounces	140 grams		
8 ounces	228 grams		
10 ounces	280 grams		
15 ounces	425 grams		
16 ounces (1 pound)	454 grams		

INDEX

ACKNOWLEDGMENTS

I am grateful for the numerous friends and family who have encouraged me to write this book, and who stood by me as I finally got it published.

To Phil and Connie, two of my biggest supporters: I could not have done this without you.

Michele Dion is the best cookie decorator I know. She also does amazing cakes at her business, Gimme Some Sugar (http://mldion .wix.com/gimme-some-sugar).

Rob Conley, owner of Beanilla.com, thank you for making some of the best extracts ever!

Mark Mason, you pushed me and got me to the finish line. Thank you.

OTHER STOREY COOKBOOKS
YOU WILL ENJOY

101 PERFECT CHOCOLATE CHIP COOKIES
by Gwen Steege

THE BAKING ANSWER BOOK
by Lauren Chattman

COOKIE CRAFT
by Valerie Peterson & Janice Fryer

FRESH MADE SIMPLE
by Lauren K. Stein; illustrated by Katie Eberts

These and other books from Storey Publishing are available wherever quality books are sold or by calling 1-800-441-5700. Visit us at *www.storey.com* or sign up for our newsletter at *www.storey.com/signup.*